Fortune Cookies

Volume 1

Dr. Kareem Pottinger

YSD Publishing House

Library of Congress Catalog in
Publication Data

YSD PUBLISHING HOUSE
14490 Coastal Bay Circle 13204
Naples, FL. 34119

Library of Congress Catalog Card
Number:
2013934185
International Standard Book
Number 978-1-937171-11-7

Dedicated to my firstborn

YOUNGSABATH POTTINGER

If I ever leave this planet, I have
always kept you in mind.

Not leavening my wisdom far behind

Grow Good

INTRODUCTION

The true intent of this book
was to write a set of guidelines
that could be
immediately implemented in
the progress and advancement
of my sons elite
life.
This vast deep knowledge was
to be used as a
tool
to keep him far beyond just,
"ahead of the learning curb" for
lack of better expression.
These
rules are the widely accepted
and used unspoken
secrets amongst the elite in
which we use to rear our

young.
Although these are our
secrets
and most of us will and should
be extremely displeased for
having them on display for the
"normal's" of the world to
receive, I decided to release
them nevertheless.
For,
upon reading the finished
piece I realized that these elite
secrets
could not only serve to benefit
my son and family to come
well, but that the entire
world
could serve to benefit from
these lists of guidelines.
The way that this book is
intended to be received is to

It
is only through the true
belief
and usage of these
guidelines
that your life's
works will be greatly
affected
in its progress.

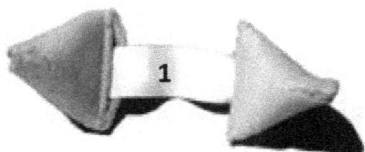

You should want to celebrate your life every moment that you get the chance to because it is the best-gift ever given to you

2

*Just
because
its
status-quo
does
not
mean
that
it is
the
correct
thing to do*

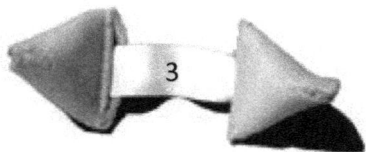

In life
you must
make
a
statement
or
else
was
your
life
really
worth it

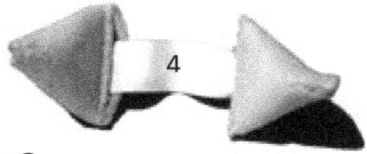

If
you are
not a part
of
the
solution
then you
very well
might be a part
of
the
problem

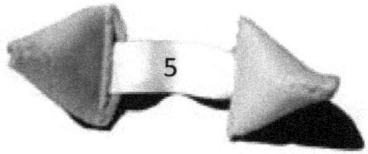

Always be careful when making decisions because you will have to live with the choices that you have made

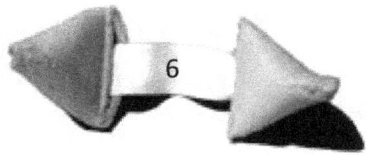

*If
you are
to make it
big in this
world
you have
to be
willing
to
make it on
your
own*

Trusting
none
leaves
no
room
for
betrayal
by
any

The bigger
the bite
that you
take
out
of your
goal,
will
always
be
what is
best

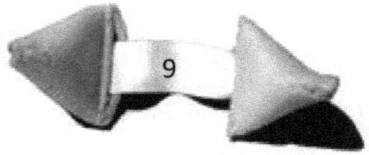

*It is very
important not to
miss your
opportunity
because
you never
know
when or if
one
will ever
come
back-around*

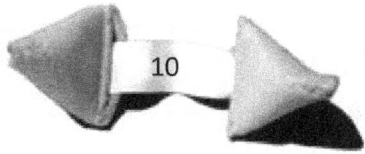

When you have
fallen-down
you have
already
accomplished
the hardest-part
towards your
goal now
there is nothing
left for you to do
but to
get back-up
and start again

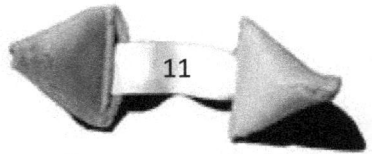

When there
is
darkness
in
your
future
it is
up to you
to
look
for the
light

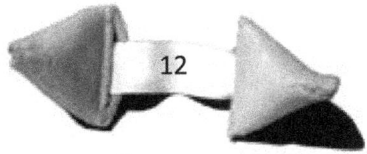

*In life you have
to learn how to
expect
the
unexpected
and
figure-out
how
to
roll
with
things*

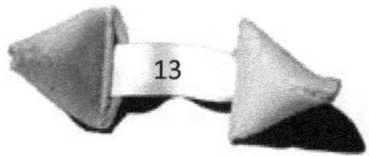

*When
it is right
there for
you to acquire
it, you
must grab a
hold of
it or
run the risk
of
becoming
regretful*

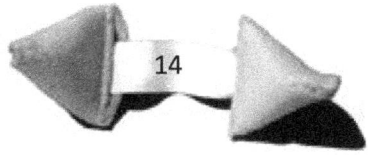

The
returning
sun
will
always
bring
other
options
for you
to
choose
from

15

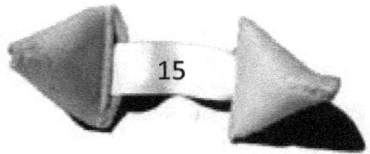

*With the
combination of
both mind and
dedication
there will be
nothing
that is
impossible
for you to
acquire
or
accomplish*

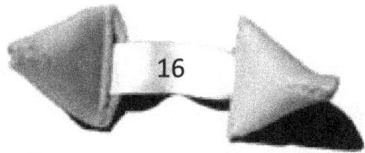

*In order to
catch a person
that is
faster
than you,
you must
force
that
person
to make
a
mistake*

*When you
learn that
life
flows in an
annual rhythm
whether
wet or dry,
it will broaden
your
perspective
on
things*

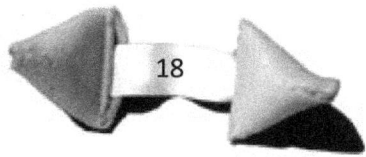

*It is always
a
great-idea
to
have
an
insurance
policy
section
in
your
planning*

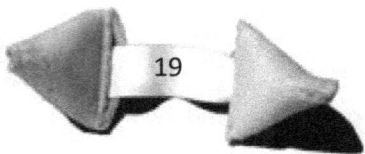

*The steep
slopes
that you
climb
in life
become
sanctuaries
once
you have
made it
to
the top*

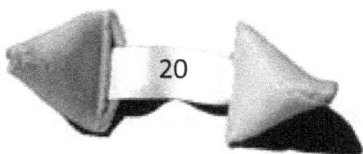

You will

never

lose

a

battle

when

you

do

not

underestimate

your

opponent

*In
life
you
have
to
give
your
ideas
a
chance
to
develop*

When your
life
becomes
a
tight rope
you
have
to
learn
how
to
balance

Looking
is
for
free
but
touching
will
always
cost
you

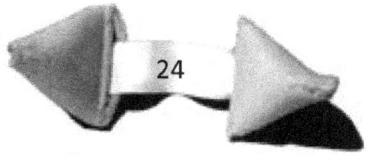

*Don't
ever
underestimate
the
fact
that
some
people
are
just
morons*

The best way to learn is by doing

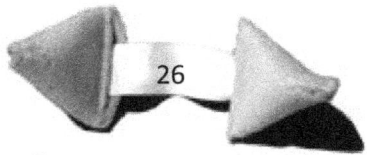

If
you don't
quit
when the
going
gets tough
then
you will not
have
anything
to
regret

*Money
won
spends
a
lot
faster
than
money
earned*

*When
it
looks
too good
to be
true
that is
when
you need to be
careful and
pay
close attention*

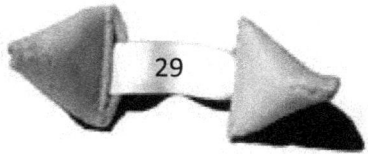

Never double-cross a person who knows your secrets

*In whatever
it is
that you
are doing
it is
important
to
know
"the ins" and
"the outs"
both back
and forth*

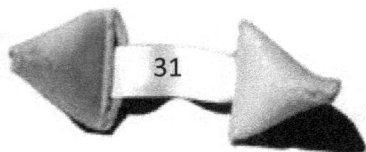

You
can be a
great
opponent
but
sometimes
there
comes a
time
when you
must
retreat

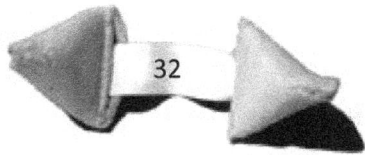

*Always keep in
mind that
you
may not
always be
playing
on the same
playing field
as the
people that you
are involved
with*

33

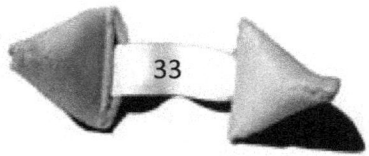

*Some people
are not
built
to be
a
follower
their
either
a
leader
or a
loner*

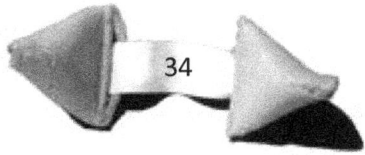

Hind
sight
is
equal
to
perfect
foresight

*You
should never
try to take
the
stripes
off of
a
zebra
because
it
cannot
be done*

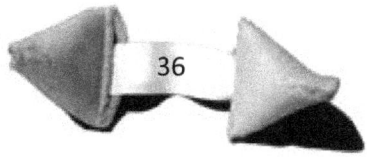

*Sometimes
you
have to
smile
at people
even
though
you would
like
to
choke
them*

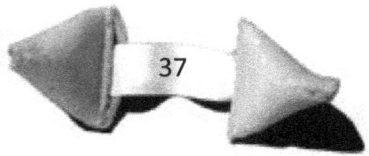

*The
crueler
the
altercation
is
the
sooner
it
will
be
over*

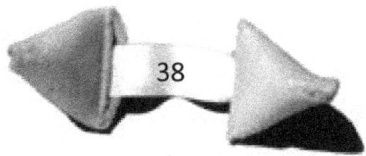

*From
a
person's
lifestyle
you
can
tell
where
they are
going
to
end-up*

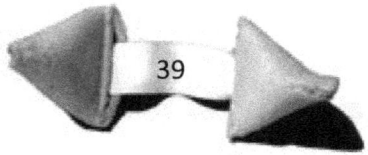

It is
a very
rewarding
experience for
you
to be out there
in the world
playing
the
game of life
and
winning

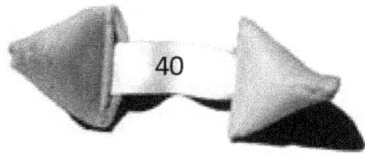

*You
cannot
score
a
homerun
without
at
least
swinging
the
bat*

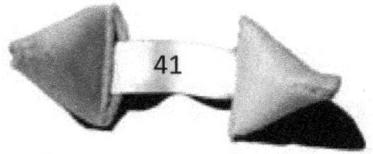

*Sometimes
what
you
are
looking
for
is right
in
front
of
your
face*

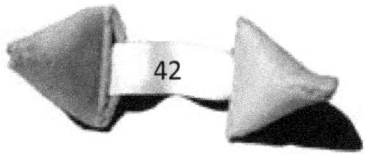

*A
wise
person
takes
full
advantage
of
an
opportunity
when
presented*

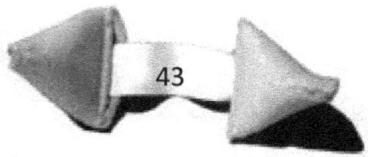

*Your life
and
its
positioning
should always
be
what is
most
important to
you
at
all times*

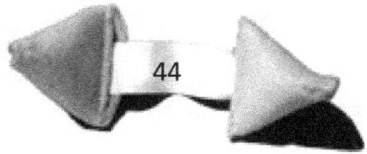

You should not have to understand the process once the outcome is great

44

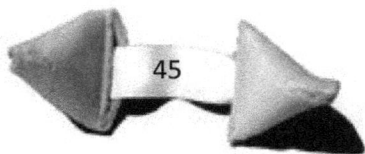

*If
you
do not
evolve
when given
the
opportunity
too,
you are
selling
yourself
short*

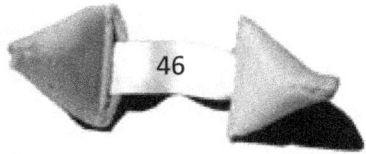

*Being
realistic
when
pacing
yourself
will
always
work-out
in
your
best
interest*

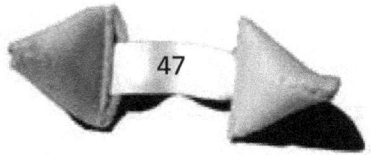

*Sometimes
it will
all
come
together
for you
in
the
last-moments;
especially
when you stick
with-it*

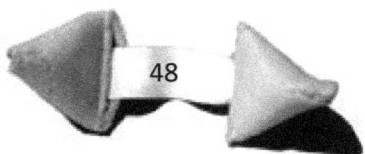

*If you
are unsatisfied
with what you
have
achieved
thus far
now
would be the
time to do
something
about
it*

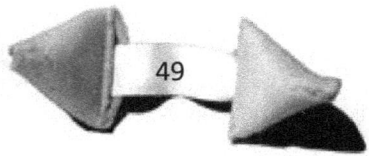

*You are
where
you
are
because
of
how
you are
and
not who
you
are*

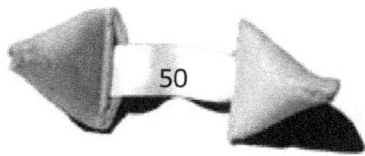

*You can
aspire
to be
like
someone else
but
always
remember that
you were
born
to be
yourself*

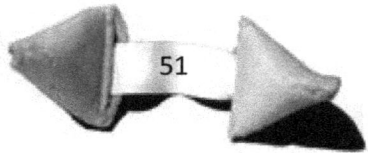

*It is not about
right
and
wrong,
it is
about
what
works for you
and
what
doesn't
work for you*

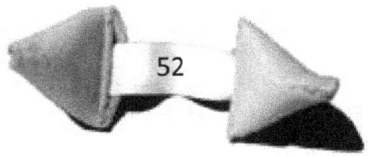

It's
better to
take
a second longer
and to do
things correct
than
a second
less and
to do
them
incorrectly

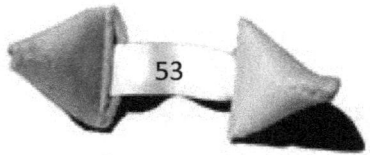

Separating
and
sectioning
is
very
important
in
life

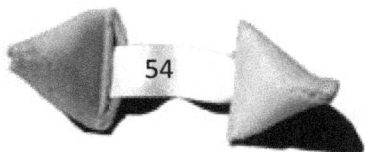

*Sometimes
you just know
certain things
deep-down
in your
bones
without ever
being warned or
told, and these
are the feelings
that you need to
pay closest
attention to*

*Do not let
the
fear
of being
discovered
the
fear of being
exposed
hold you
back from
accomplishing
your dreams*

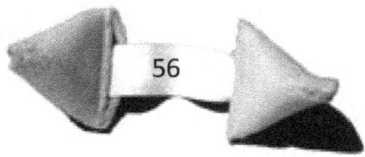

*The
weak
ones;
be very aware
that they
do
perish
along
the
way
of
obtaining-goals*

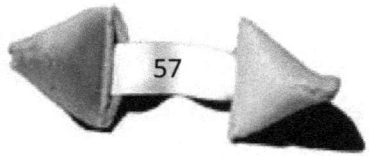

Continuous
adjustments
in
your
small-moves
will
and
do
lead
to
big-moves

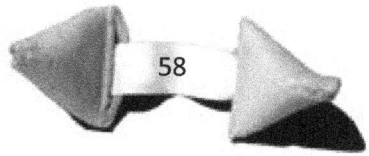

*The
simplest
explanation
is
usually
the
right
one*

*Success
is
not
final
and
failure
is
not
fatal*

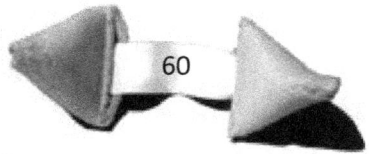

*A
positive
thought
leaves
a
positive
imprint*

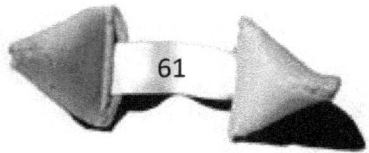

*Talk
is
no
substitute
for
action*

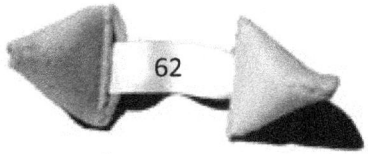

In regards to your own agenda; you are responsible for making it happen and no-one else

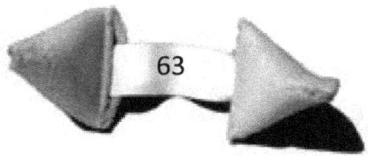

After a while

a

picture

starts to

emerge

of

just how

effective

whatever

your

doing

has become

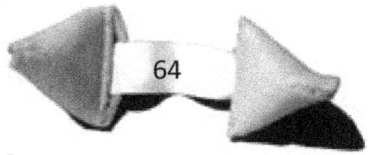

A
negative
thought
will
leave
a
negative
imprint

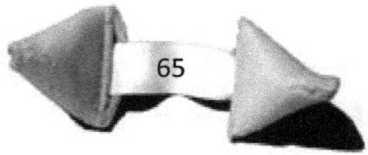

*It
will always
be
in
your
best-interest
to
learn
all
you can
while
you can*

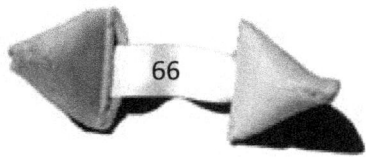

*There
will
always
be
a
difference
between
the
haves
and
the
have-not's*

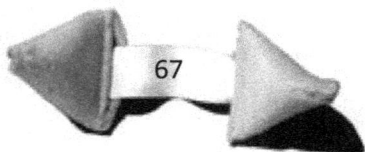

*Second
guessing
yourself,
does
not
work*

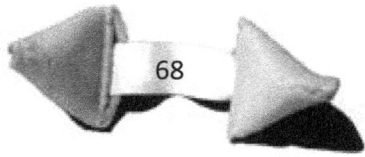

*When
your
taking
the
risk
is
usually
when
your
closest
to
success*

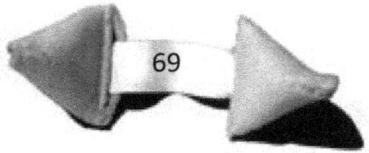

*When
you decide to
take a
chance; you
must be
willing
to
take
whatever
comes
with that
chance*

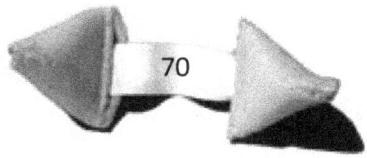

*You shouldn't
try to
fool yourself;
either
you
like it
or
you
don't,
it is
just that
simple*

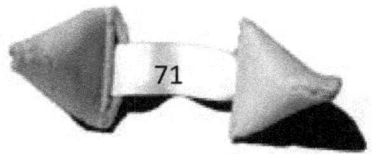

*It is
very
important
to
your
success
too
know
where
you
need to
grow*

72

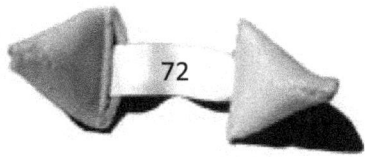

As
such
is
the
rules;
such
will
be
the
game

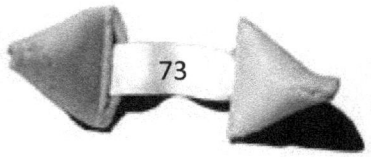

*Only when you
are able to
change
your
way
of
thinking
will you be able
to
change
your way of
life*

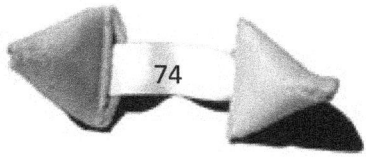

*The world
is
made in
a
perfect-balance
when one
door
shuts
another
one
will always
swing-open*

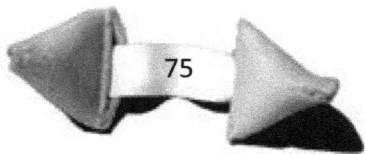

*Your
version
of
perfect
and
their
version
of
perfect
might
be
different*

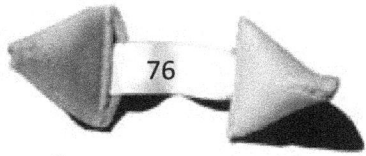

*Sometimes
you only
get
one
chance
to
accomplish
something
and
one
chance
only*

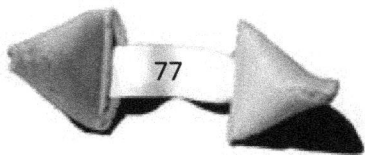

*In life,
sometimes
it's
do
it
right
the
first-time
or
not
at
all*

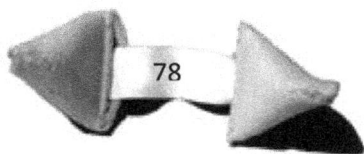

*The past
should be a
strange place;
when you
go back
it is not
suppose
to
recognize
you and if it
does, you
haven't grown*

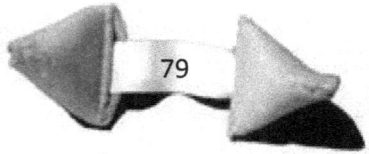

*There's
a
huge world
out
there
for you
to go
and see,
so don't get
stuck
in
one-spot*

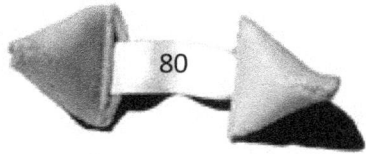

*Even when
you have
a
setback
there will
always
be a
comeback
somewhere;
you
just have to
find it*

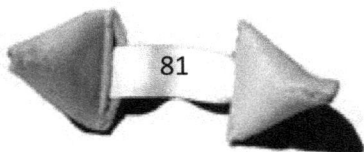

*Most times
all you
need
to
do
is
just
reach-out
there
and
grab
it*

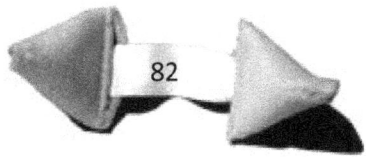

Quality-work
takes
time,
you
have
to
prepare
yourself
to
get
better

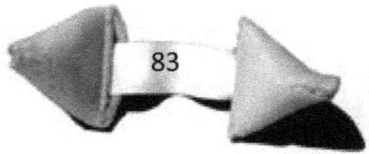

*Be
aware
that
when
times
change
so
will
your
financial
needs*

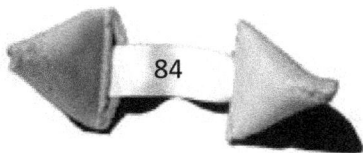

*You
have to
think
big
and
do
big
in
order
to
become
big*

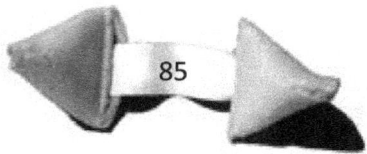

*What
separates
the successful
from the
unsuccessful
is simply
who
handles
it in the line
of fire
and who
doesn't*

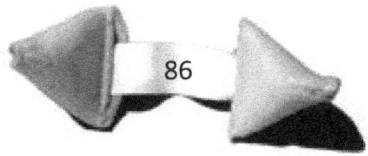

*You should
always keep in
mind that many
people
work
for a long
time
to get to
the position
that
their currently
in*

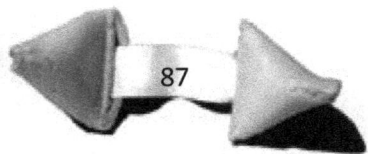

*Remember
that
some
people
are
most
comfortable
being
a
loser;
it is
easier*

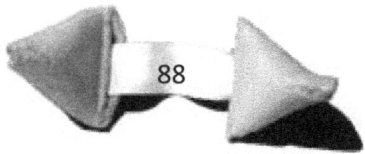

When you are out there in the world achieving just remember that you're out there achieving to better your life

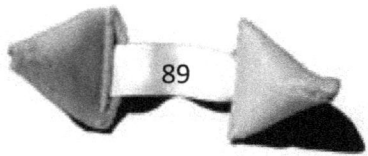

If
it's
not
going
to
work-out
it's
not
going
to
work-out

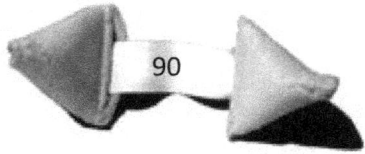

When your life becomes harder, you will have to become stronger

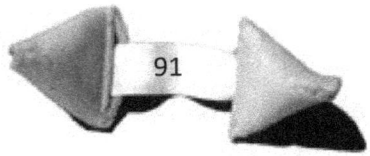

*The
winning team
is going
to laugh
and
have
a
great-time,
while
the
losing team
is not*

92

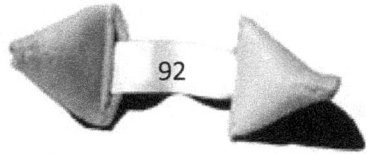

*Life's
filled
with
both small
and
large
challenges,
don't
get
consumed
by the small
ones*

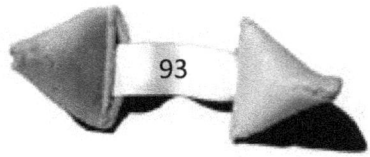

*If your
not
doing
anything
to be
remembered by
then
you are running
the risk of
becoming
a
nobody*

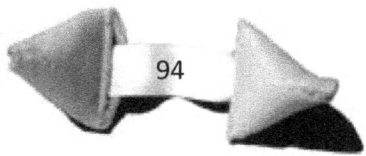

*Life
is a
continuous
creation
in
which
you have
to do
what you
have too,
in
order to
evolve*

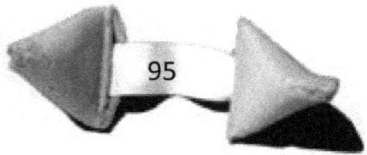

When
you use both
truth and logic
as
your
guide
you
can
never
be
steered
wrong

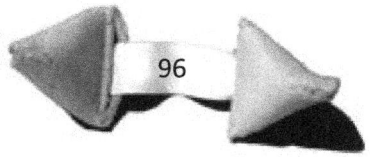

*Almost
every
day
above
ground
should
be
thought
of
as
a
privilege*

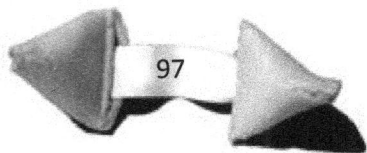

*In this
life
you will
either
evolve
or
retard,
and
when you are
not evolving
you are
retarding*

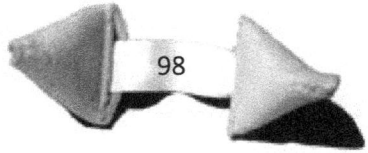

*Being
overly
ambitious
when
there
are
time-restraints
may
cause
an
unnecessary
problem*

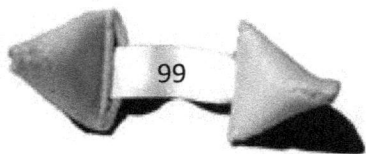

With a little bit
of
hard-work
and
sweat,
there
is
nothing
that
cannot
be
obtained

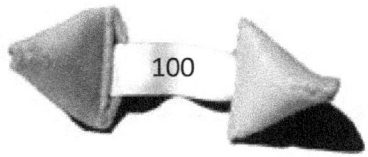

*You can
tell
when
someone
has
been
working
because
you
can see
their
progress*

*You have to
make
money
with
the
good-hands
while
you
have them;
that is
why you have
them*

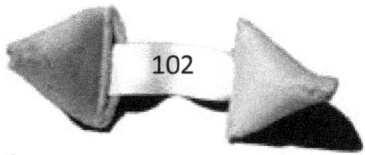

*What
you
cannot
chase
and
catch,
you
have
to
trap*

*It is
up to
you
to
decide
who
you are
and
will
become
in
life*

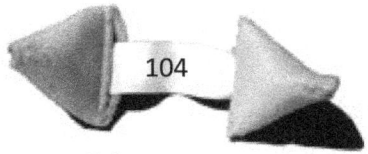

*Do not allow
doubt
to seep in
upon
trying
to
accomplish a
task
or else
you will not
accomplish that
task*

Sometimes
we
go
to
drink
from
the
well,
one
too
many
times

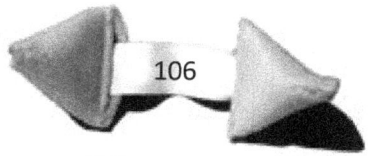

*We all
are
going
to be
responsible
for
what
we
do;
sooner
or
later*

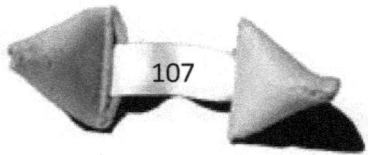

It's important not to forget about the little people when climbing the latter, because that is who you will see again if you were to go back down

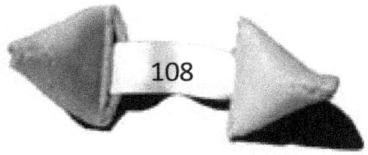

The
conflict
never
ends
with
a
contentious
person
so
don't
even
start

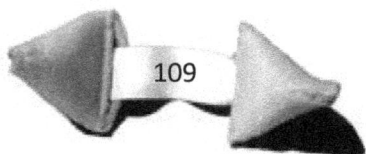

*When
you don't have
that many
lines
in the
script,
you must
say
the ones
that
you have
very well*

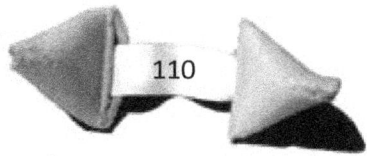

*Sometimes
you
just
have
to
keep
things
simple;
get-in
and
get-it
done*

With some
words,
you
have
to be
very
careful
when you
choose
to
speak
them

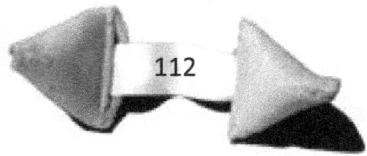

*There
is a reason
and a purpose
why your life
is the way
it is
and
finding out
why
will always
better
your situation*

*True
love
might
switch
gears
but
it
never
dies*

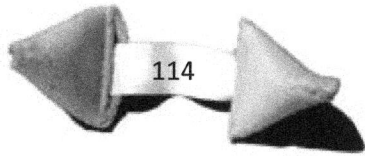

*At
the end
of it
all,
you can't
slow-down
the
people
that are
in
the
right*

*Earning
large
dollars
will
lead
to
having
large
times*

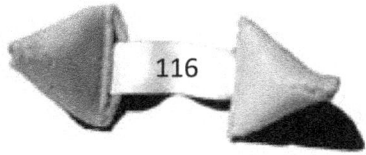

*As human-
beings we will
all have our
ups
and
we all
have
our
downs, the
point is to learn
from them
both*

Unless
your
using some
kind
of
strategy,
you
should
always
play
to
win

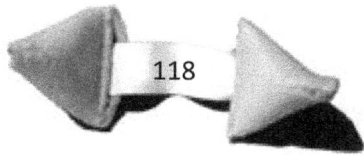

When moving forward is no longer simple and
starts to become tough; only the lowly will choose to
walk-out of the door, rather than sticking it out and following through

*Once
you have
found
your
center
it will
be
hard
for you
to
get
lost*

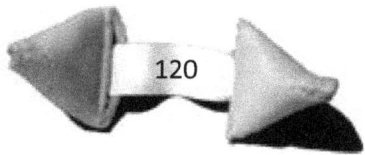

When
you
see
smoke
you
should
prepare
for
fire

*You
will never
get to
the
top
of
your
game
by
making
dumb
decisions*

*Any
life
worthwhile,
is
not
going
to
be
cheap*

Even when you are hungry, you have to be cautious about putting too much onto your plate

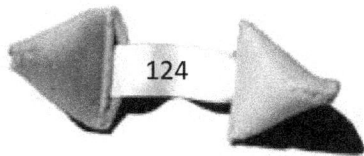

Sometimes
you may get
yourself into
a
position
where
you
either
fold
or
get
rolled-over

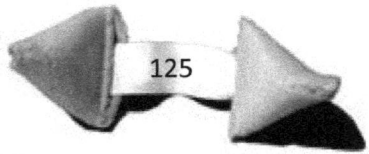

*The
easier
the
metal bends
the harder
it will be
to
weld
after
you
have
broken-it*

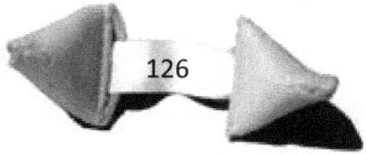

*Great
fetes of
engineering
never
start-out at the
top;
they start
from the
bottom and
work
their way
up*

*When you're
not as
smart
as you
think
you are,
you
turn
yourself
into
a
liability*

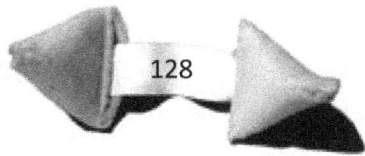

*Every once
in a while
you have to
step out of
your comfort
zone and push
yourself
to the limit
in order
to see how far
you can
go*

*When
you go
high-enough
you will
always
come to
one
person
who is
in charge
of it
all*

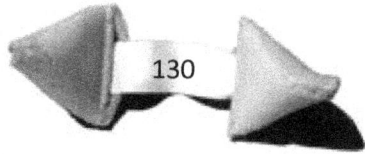

When

you

keep-up

the

good-work

the

good-work

will

definitely

keep

you

up

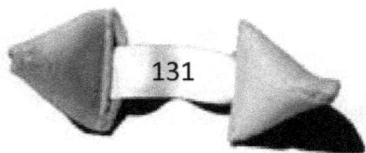

There
can
be
no
excuses
when
you
are
the
leader

132

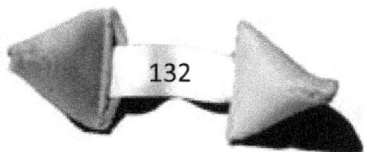

Sometimes
just
taking
a
breather
is
what
is
best

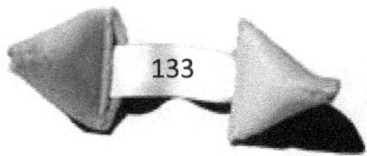

*Some people
will
always
choose
not to
listen
and
there is
nothing
that
you can do
about it*

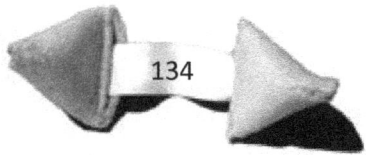

When seeking
information
about a
person,
you cannot
dig
any
deeper
than
a
person's
ex-spouse

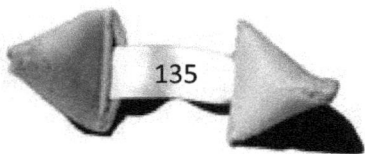

As long as you refuse to settle, keep trying and you will succeed

When you
always
make
room
for the
unexpected
you
will always
have the
space
to fix
a mistake

*What can you
do today
that will help
your
life-goals
move forward
is a very
good
question
to
ask
yourself*

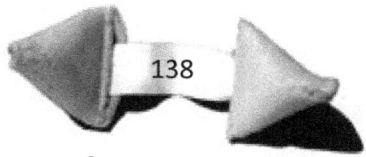

You can always
go further
than you think
you can, you
just have to
figure out
what
will it
take
to give you
that
extra push

139

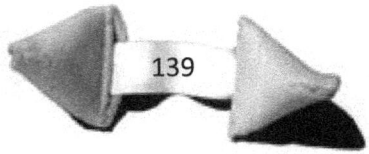

*You can not
escape
the fact that
there will
always be
risk,
it just matters
if the
risk are
acceptable
or
not*

140

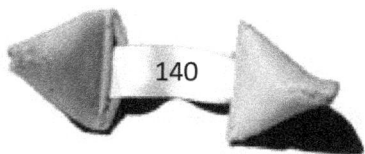

*Sometimes
in order
to
succeed
all
you
have to
do is
make a
few
small
adjustments*

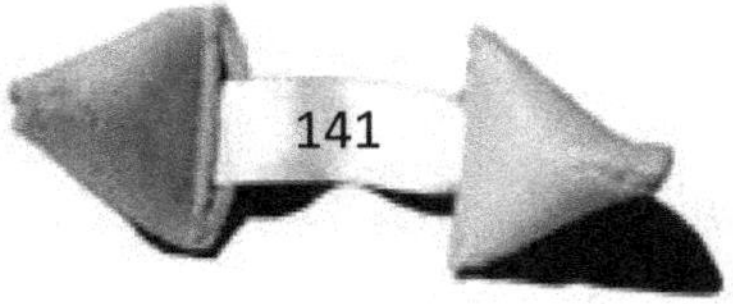

*Don't
forget
that
in
life
you
should
always
cut
your
angles*

142

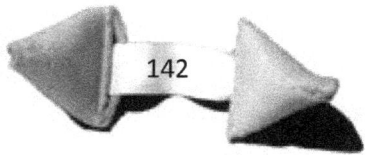

*Why
swim
up-stream
when
its
easier
to
swim
down-stream*

143

*Always
do the best
that
you can
with what
you have
and the
rest
will take
care
of
itself*

144

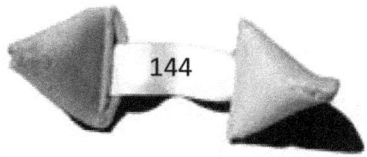

*You
will
always
be
weak
until
you
learn
how
to
take
control*

You should always keep in mind that some people posses a sense of urgency while others don't

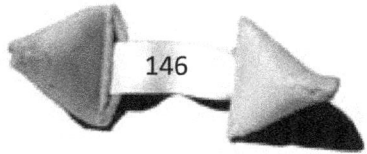

*In order
to
become a
winner
you must
do the
things
that the
losers
are
unwilling
to do*

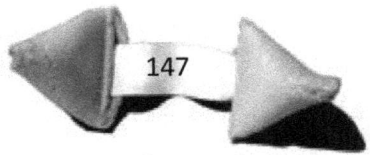

A lot of
the
times
you will
only
need to
reassess
your
game-plan
in order
to
win

*Revenge
is
like
a
poison,
it
will
turn
you
into
something
ugly*

*A
good
deceiver
makes
you
believe
their
lie*

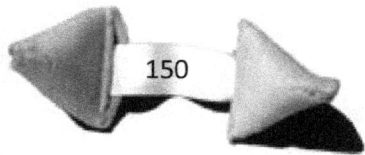

Life's
like a
river,
you
have
to
go
where
it
will
take
you

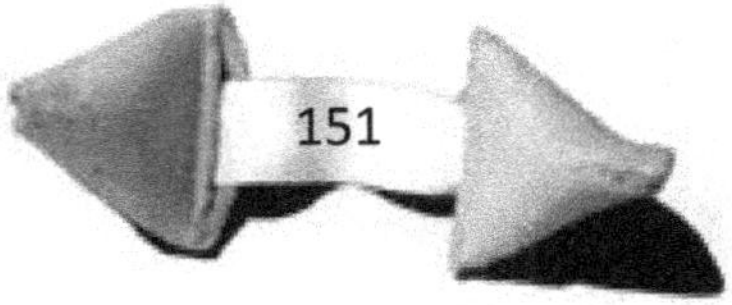

151

*Desperate
people
will
make
mistakes,
mistakes
that
you
can
benefit
from*

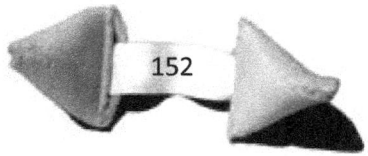

*You
have
to
work
hard
in
order
to
make
luck
happen*

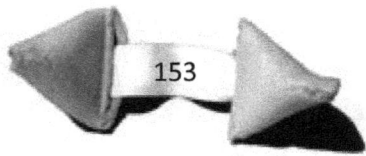

*When you don't
know
what you're
going to do
next,
it's a good idea
to take
a step-back
and
ask
for
advice*

*When you
really
do
believe
in
yourself,
you
can
achieve
anything
that
you want*

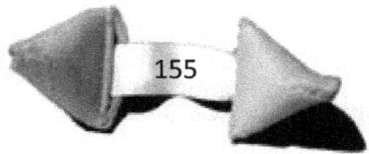

*Temporary
solutions
will
only
hold
you
back*

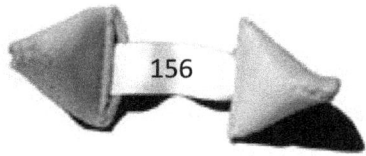

If you are not careful, your dreams and aspirations can get pushed to the side by everyday life

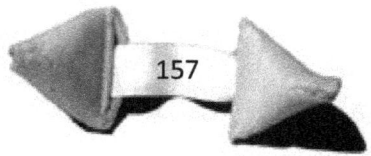

*Never
become
a
victim
of
your
own
life*

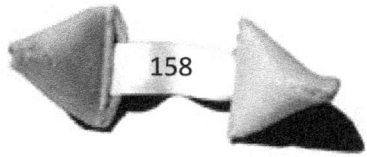

When

you

are

truly

lucky

you

don't

out

live

love

The end

Additional books written by
Dr. Kareem Pottinger available online at
www.FORTUNECOOKIES.me
and your local book stores nationwide

FORTUNE COOKIES VOLUMES 1-11

also

available

on

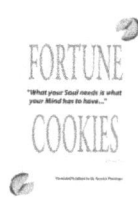
your

Kindle

Nook

Apple

devices